GREYSCALE THEATRE COMPANY

GODS ARE FALLEN AND ALL SAFETY GONE / A PRAYER

by Selma Dimitrijevic

1

GREYSCALE is a Newcastle based international theatre company formed by a group of established directors, writers, actors, and designers interested in exploring the fringes and gaps in-between the ways we work. We aim to make carefully structured, powerfully live, political and anarchic theatre for a modern audience bored of being bored.

We work in a number of different ways but mostly like the idea that everyone should be able to provoke a process, not just the director and the writer.

We also tend to think that the audience shouldn't get to sit in the dark snoozing, that you should enjoy our shows more than we do and that to get something out, you have to put something in. www.greyscale.org.uk

Greyscale is an UNLIMITED ALLY; celebrating the work of disabled artists as part of the Unlimited programme. www.weareunlimited.org.uk

GREYSCALE ENSEMBLE: Selma Dimitrijevic, Lorne Campbell, Oliver Townsend, Sean Campion, Scott Turnbull, Leo Warner, Mark Grimmer, Jon Bausor, Garance Marneur, Sandy Grierson, David Ireland, Jimmy Akingbola, Elspeth Brodie and Gary Collins.

GODS ARE FALLEN AND ALL SAFETY GONE

GODS ARE FALLEN AND ALL SAFETY GONE was first commissioned and presented by David MacLennan for **A Play, A Pie and A Pint** 2007 season and directed by Pamela Carter.

In 2009 the play was presented at **"Lyubimovka" Festival** in Moscow and in 2010 opened in co-production between **Teatr.doc and Afisha Moscow** directed by Viktor Ryzhakov. This production won numerous awards and has transferred to Meyerhold Centre in 2014.

Development of GREYSCALE's version of the show was supported by **Almeida** theatre and NRTF showcase and this version was first presented at Almeida Festival in 2012.

In 2014 GODS ARE FALLEN ... was part of caravan international showcase, PULSE festival, IGNITE festival and in 2015 is embarking on an 8 week UK tour and taking part in British Council Showcase 2015.

GODS COMPANY

SELMA DIMITRIJEVIC (writer and director)

Director, playwright and Artistic Director of *Greyscale* Selma has worked in theatre, film and opera in a wide range of styles, traditions and forms. Her plays have been performed in the UK, Canada, Russia, Ukraine and Croatia. As a director she has worked with theatres such as Northern Stage, Theatre Royal Bath, Dundee Rep, Traverse, Tron, Stellar Quines, Hull Truck and Almeida and as a collaborator with theatre makers such as Caroline Horton, RashDash and Gary Kitching and Co.

Selma is on the board of Newcastle based theatre company *Open Clasp* and Alex Swift's theatre company *Permanent Red*.

OLIVER TOWNSEND (designer)

Oli studied painting before training in theatre design at the Royal Welsh College of Music and Drama. Other work with Greyscale includes *The Chekhov Project*, *The Gamblers*, *Dead To Me*, and *A Beginning, A Middle, and An End*. In 2014 he was awarded Best Set Designer at the Off West End Awards for *Grounded* (Gate Theatre). Oli has designed shows for RashDash, Caroline Horton & Company, The Bush Theatre, The Lyric Hammersmith, The Gate Theatre, The Traverse, Nabokov, Newcastle Live, Royal & Derngate, Gary Kitching & Company, The Royal Court, Hampstead Theatre, Scottish Opera, Blackheath Halls Opera, English National Opera, English Touring Opera, Druid Theatre, The Union Theatre, Opera Up Close, and Alexander Whitley Dance Company. He lives in London and is an Associate Artist of the Gate Theatre.

SCOTT TURNBULL (Daughter)

Scott's theatre credits include *Get Santa* (Northern Stage), *Time and the Conways* (Nottingham Playhouse), *The Noise* (Unlimited Theatre) *Gods are Fallen and All Safety Gone* (Greyscale), *Rhetoric* (Greyscale), *Harmless Creatures* (Greyscale), *The Rubber Room* (The Old Vic), *The Machine Gunners* (Polka Theatre), *Apples* (Northern Stage), *The Tempest* (KG Productions), *Book of Beasts* (Catherine Wheels Theatre Company), *Hansel and Gretel* (Northern Stage), *Heartbreak Soup* (Empty Space Productions), *A Christmas Carol* (Northern Stage) and *How Many Miles to Basra?* (The West Yorkshire Playhouse). His television credits include *Little Bastard* (Baby Cow), *The Royal Today, The Bill* (TalkBack Thames) and *Byker Grove*. He was chosen by *The Independent* as 'One to Watch' in 2011 and was awarded North-East Actor of the Year by *The Journal*. He is also a continuity announcer for Sky Television.

SEAN CAMPION (Mother)

Theatre includes *King Lear* (Abbey Theatre), *Witteberg* (Gate Theatre), *Observe the sons of Ulsters marching towards the Somme* (Abbey Theatre), *Death and The Maiden* and *Othello* (Salisbury Theatre), *The Quare Fellow* (Trycycle Theatre), *Mutabilitie, Tarry Flynn* (Royal National Theatre).

Sean was nominated both for Olivier award in the West End and Tony award on Broadway for his role as Jake Quinn in *Stones in His Pockets*. Television includes Series 1 & 2 of *Borgia, Vera* (ITV) and *Mr Selfridge* (ITV).

Characters:

Anne (mother) .... Sean Campion

Annie (daughter)............................. Scott Turnbull

Scene 1

Mother's house. Front room. Her room.
There is a comfortable chair and a few blankets.
Small table near. A few mugs, newspapers, glasses, TV schedule and a pair
of socks scattered around the room.
It's a comfortable, warm place.
Mother is in her chair, asleep.
She is holding a cup of tea.
Annie comes in.
She just had a nice, long bath.
Annie goes to her Mum and gently tries taking a cup of tea from her hand.
Mum wakes up.

MUM   Oh.

ANNIE   Sorry. I didn't mean to wake you up.

MUM   I wasn't asleep.

ANNIE   Can I take the …

MUM   I'm not done yet.

ANNIE   Oh. Okay.

MUM   Have you had your bath?

ANNIE   Yes.

MUM   Was there enough hot water?

ANNIE   Yes, there was plenty.

MUM   Did you piss in the shower again?

ANNIE   No. Of course I didn't.

MUM   I'm just asking.

ANNIE   I never do that.

MUM   It's a cunt to clean, you know.

ANNIE   Sorry?

MUM   It's hard to clean.

ANNIE   Right.

MUM   Come here.

ANNIE   What?

MUM   Come here.

Mum spits on her thumb and wipes ANNIE'S face.

ANNIE   What is it?

MUM   Toothpaste. There.

ANNIE   Thank you.

MUM   That's better.

ANNIE   Where's Dad gone?

MUM   How would I know? You think he tells me anything?

ANNIE   He just disappeared.

MUM   That's your Dad for you.

ANNIE   I wanted to talk to him.

MUM   Maybe next time.

ANNIE   Always "next time".

MUM   What did they say about the weather?

ANNIE   Who?

MUM   On the radio.

ANNIE   Some rain I think. Cloudy. Nothing too bad.

MUM   Tz, tz, tz.

ANNIE   -
          What?

MUM   It'll kill the crops.

ANNIE   Will it now?

MUM   Oh yes.

ANNIE   And what do you know about crops?

MUM   I know what kills them. Rain and strong winds. Kills
          them. Just like that.

ANNIE   It's April, Mum, bit of rain is just fine.

MUM   You'll see once they're all dead. Just you wait.

ANNIE   I saw aunt Marie this morning.

MUM   Did you?

ANNIE   Yes.

MUM   And. Is she well?

ANNIE   Well, no.
         -
         How could she be?

MUM   What's wrong now?

ANNIE   Didn't she tell you?

MUM   Tell me what?

ANNIE   Someone broke into their house.

MUM   When?

ANNIE   Last night.

MUM   See. No one tells me anything.

ANNIE   She left you a message.

MUM   No she didn't.

ANNIE   Well she said she did.

MUM   Where?

ANNIE	On your answering machine.
MUM	Ach.
ANNIE	Didn't you hear it?
MUM	I heard the phone.
ANNIE	And?
MUM	It was ringing all bloody evening.
ANNIE	So why didn't you answer then?
MUM	Your Dad wasn't here.
ANNIE	So what?
MUM	You know I don't like answering the phone when your Dad is not around. Besides, it was late, who knows who was it.
ANNIE	It was aunt Marie.
MUM	Well I didn't know that, did I?
ANNIE	Well if you answered the phone you'd know.
MUM	I don't know. All that stuff they've got. It's just asking for trouble.
ANNIE	Luckily the burglars didn't take anything.
MUM	So why call me then in the middle of the night.

ANNIE   I don't know, I think she just got a fright.

MUM   And you went to see her?

ANNIE   Yes, Mark and I stopped by this morning. You know, to see if there is anything we can do.

MUM   Like what?

ANNIE   I don't know, check if they are all right, maybe tidy up a bit.

MUM   And you need Mark to tidy up?

ANNIE   No, I didn't need him, but it was nice of him to come.

MUM   Didn't he have to go to work?

ANNIE   Mum.

MUM   What?

ANNIE   It's Sunday.

MUM   But if it wasn't …

ANNIE   -

MUM   He does have a job to go to, doesn't he?

ANNIE   No, he doesn't.

MUM   How come?

ANNIE   You know very well how come.

MUM   Remind me.

ANNIE   He's looking for a job.

MUM   Is he?

ANNIE   Yes, he is.

MUM   Oh I don't know. He could've found one by now.

ANNIE   He is looking for the right one.

MUM   Ach.

ANNIE   What?

MUM   Can't you find someone else dear?

ANNIE   Mum.

MUM   What?

ANNIE   Well, you know, I kind of like Mark.

MUM   But he doesn't make any money.

ANNIE   He made loads, and we have enough now, he's just not working *at the moment*, but we are fine.

MUM   Ach.

ANNIE   Trust me. We have enough.

MUM   That place you live in…

ANNIE   It's perfectly nice.

MUM   It doesn't have a bath.

ANNIE   We have a shower.

MUM   But not a bath.

ANNIE   Mum, just say it, if you mind / me taking

MUM   You know, sometimes I really feel sorry for you, never
         learned to fight for yourself, did you, and now look
         (where you are), poor thing, having to come all the way
         here ...

ANNIE   I'm coming to see *you*. Not to have a bath. It's just that
         you / always fall

MUM   So what did she say?

ANNIE   Who?

MUM   Aunt Marie, who else. Is she happy now?

ANNIE   Why would she be happy?

MUM   Now she'll have something new to moan about.

ANNIE   Mum.

MUM   We'll never hear the end of that. I'm telling you. All
         she ever does is talk about herself. It's all me, me, me.
         You know, I don't understand that, people talking about
         themselves all the time.

ANNIE   That's not really true Mum.

MUM   And I tell her. Don't think I don't. I tell her when she
          starts. That's why she doesn't like me.

ANNIE   She absolutely loves you.

MUM   So did she ask about me? About my chest?

ANNIE   She was still in shock.

MUM   Yes. I'm sure she was.

ANNIE   The police were there. They can't figure out how
          anyone got in.

MUM   She should just go over and ask them.

ANNIE   Ask who?

MUM   You know who.

ANNIE   No … I don't.

MUM   Them, you know, from across the street. I'm sure they
          are quite capable of picking a lock.

ANNIE   Mum. Please.

MUM   I'm just saying.

ANNIE   They are a nice family.

MUM   And how would you know, you don't understand a
          word they say. You can't even talk to them.

ANNIE   They speak perfectly good English.

MUM   When it suits them. Only when it suits them …

ANNIE   I think it's time you go and see them.

MUM   See who?

ANNIE   Aunt and uncle.

MUM   Ach. I'm too tired.

ANNIE   You could do it just fine.

MUM   I can't.

ANNIE   Why not?

MUM   I have this … here. You know. Like it's stuck. All the
        time now.
        Like I need to wash it down.

ANNIE   Well I'm sure they would let you have some water. Or
        tea. Or coffee.

MUM   Ach. (I don't know.)

ANNIE   Or anything else you might want to have.

MUM   Like it's stuck. Right here. Here. Like … ugh.

ANNIE   Should you go and see a doctor then?

MUM   What do they know?

ANNIE   I don't know. More then we do?

MUM   Nah. It's just … you know. Right here. Like glue. Here.
            Makes it hard to … breathe.

ANNIE   Is there anything I can do?

MUM   No, no. It's nothing for you to worry about.

ANNIE   How about tea? Would a cup of tea help a little bit?

MUM   Oh I don't know.

ANNIE   Mum.

MUM   I don't know. Maybe.

ANNIE   Yes? No?

MUM   Only if you are making it.

ANNIE   -
            I am, yes.

MUM   Oh that would be nice.

ANNIE   Can I take that one?

ANNIE tries to take a mug from MUM'S hand.

MUM   I'm not finished yet.

ANNIE   Fine. (I'll be) back in a second.

ANNIE leaves to make the tea.

MUM   And don't forget the sugar, Annie, don't forget the sugar, yes?

Mother keeps looking to where Annie disappeared.

Scene 2

Mother is in the chair, she fell asleep.
She is still holding a cup of tea.
Annie comes in.
She just had a nice, long bath.
Annie goes to her Mum and tries gently taking a cup of tea from her hands.
Mum wakes up.

MUM   Oh.

ANNIE   Sorry. I didn't mean to wake you up.

MUM   I wasn't asleep.

ANNIE   Can I take the …

MUM   I'm not done yet.

ANNIE   Oh. Okay.

MUM   Have you had your bath?

ANNIE   Yes.

MUM   Was there enough hot water?

ANNIE   Yes, there was plenty.

MUM   Did you piss in the shower again?

ANNIE   No. Of course I didn't.

MUM   I'm just asking.

ANNIE   I never do that.

MUM   It's a cunt to clean, you know.

ANNIE   Mum.

MUM   It's hard to clean, I said.

ANNIE   Right.

MUM   Come here.

ANNIE   What?

MUM   Come here.

Mum spits on her finger and wipes ANNIE'S face.

ANNIE   What is it?

MUM   Toothpaste. There.

ANNIE   Thank you.

MUM   That's better.

ANNIE   Where's Dad gone?

MUM   How would I know? You think he tells me anything?

ANNIE   He just disappeared.

MUM   That's your Dad for you.

ANNIE   I wanted to talk to him.

MUM   Maybe next time.

ANNIE   Always "next time".

MUM   What did they say about the weather?

ANNIE   Who?

MUM   On the radio.

ANNIE   Hot and clear, nothing too bad I think.

MUM   Tz, tz, tz.

ANNIE   -
        What now?

MUM   It will ruin the crops. All that sun.

ANNIE   Will it now?

MUM   Oh yes.

ANNIE   And what do you know about crops?

MUM   I know what kills them. Sun.

        Sun and strong winds. Kills them. Just like that.

ANNIE   It's April, Mum, a bit of sunshine is just fine.

MUM   You'll see once it's all dead. Just you wait.

ANNIE   I saw aunt Marie last night.

MUM   Did you?

ANNIE   Yes.

MUM   And is she well?

ANNIE   She is just fine.

MUM   What's wrong?

ANNIE   Nothing.

MUM   Don't lie to me. I can tell.

ANNIE   It's nothing. Really. It's all fine now.

MUM   Finish what you started.

ANNIE   -
         Someone broke into their house.

MUM   No. When?

ANNIE   Last night.

MUM   And not a word to me. Nice.

ANNIE   She didn't want to worry you.

MUM   My own sister. Never tells me anything.

ANNIE   Well it's not a big deal.

MUM   Not even a phone call.

ANNIE   It was late and she knows you don't like people calling
           you that late at night. You probably wouldn't have
           answered anyway.

MUM   Of course I would. How can you say that?

ANNIE   Mum.

MUM   Not even a phone call. My own sister.
           See. No one tells me anything.

ANNIE   Well no one's hurt. And nothing was taken.

MUM   What could be taken, they never had anything.

ANNIE   Anyway. They are fine now.

MUM   Did Mark drive you there?

ANNIE   No.
           -
           He didn't.

MUM   How come?

ANNIE   He just didn't. All right.

MUM   What's wrong?

ANNIE   Nothing.

MUM   I don't know. That doesn't sound like Mark.
           To let you do things all on your own. Take care of your
           family like that …

ANNIE   Mum …

MUM   Well I'm just saying.

ANNIE   I don't need him to tidy up.

MUM   It's not about needing, it's about having someone around.

ANNIE   Mark and I broke up.

MUM   No-oo.

ANNIE   Well … yes.

MUM   But you are crap on your own.

ANNIE   Oh. Thanks for that Mum.

MUM   So. What was it?

ANNIE   What do you mean?

MUM   What did you do to him?

ANNIE   I didn't do anything.

MUM   Why did he leave you then?

ANNIE   Look … It's complicated.

MUM   How complicated could it be? He is a very nice young man. He must have had a reason to leave.

ANNIE   He didn't leave. It was me.

MUM   It was you - what?

ANNIE   I broke up with him.

MUM   No. You didn't.

ANNIE   Yes I did.

MUM   You don't just go around leaving people.

ANNIE   Apparently I do.

MUM   And why would you do that?

ANNIE   I told you, it's complicated.

MUM   Do you know how old you are?

ANNIE   Yes I do. Thank you.

MUM   And what are you going to do now? What will you do without him? What can you do without him?

ANNIE   I thought you didn't like him.

MUM   Now how can you say that?

ANNIE   Well somehow I was just under the impression ...

MUM   You know, you'll never find anyone as good as him, just as long as you know that.

ANNIE   I don't know about that.

MUM   He was your last chance.

ANNIE   Mum.

MUM   He buys you that nice flat and you throw him out. Just like that.

ANNIE   He didn't buy it – we did. Together. And I didn't throw him out.

MUM   So was she happy?

ANNIE   Who?

MUM   Aunt Marie, who else. You know she never liked him that much.

ANNIE   No, she liked him just fine. I think it was / you who didn't

MUM   Did she ask about him?

ANNIE   Well ... no. But she was still in shock.

MUM   They should just go and ask him about it?

ANNIE   Ask who?

MUM   That son of theirs.

ANNIE   What's he got to do with it?

MUM   Drugs.

ANNIE   Drugs what?

MUM   He needed money for drugs.

ANNIE   He is not even taking drugs.

MUM   Don't be naive. Have you seen what he looks like?

ANNIE   He is sixteen. That's what sixteen year olds look like.

MUM   And those friends of his. Ach.

ANNIE   I think you should go and see them.

MUM   See who?

ANNIE   Aunt and uncle.

MUM   No-o. I'm too tired.

ANNIE   You could do it just fine.

MUM   I can't.

ANNIE   Why not?

MUM   I have this … here. You know. Like it's stuck. All the
         time now. Like I need to wash it down.

ANNIE   Well I'm sure they would let you have some water. Or
         tea. Or coffee.

MUM   Ach. (I don't know.)

ANNIE   Or anything else you might want to have.

MUM   Like it's stuck. Right here. Here. Like … ugh.

ANNIE   Should you go and see a doctor then?

MUM   What do they know?

ANNIE   I don't know. More then we do?

MUM   Nah. It's just … you know. Right here. Like glue. Here.
          Makes it hard to … breathe.

ANNIE   Is there anything I can do?

MUM   No, no. It's nothing for you to worry about.

ANNIE   How about tea? Would a cup of tea help a little bit?

MUM   Oh I don't know.

ANNIE   Come on, Mum. Yes, no?

MUM   Only if you are making it.

ANNIE   -
          I am, yes.

MUM   Lovely.

ANNIE   Can I take that one?

MUM   I'll just finish it.

ANNIE   Fine. (I'll be) back in a second .

ANNIE leaves.

MUM   And don't forget the sugar, Annie, don't forget the
          sugar, yes?

Scene 3

Mother is in the chair, asleep.
She is still holding a cup of tea.
Annie comes in.
She just had a nice, long bath.
Annie goes to her Mum and tries gently taking a cup of tea from her hands.
Mum wakes up.

MUM   Oh.

ANNIE   Sorry. I didn't mean to wake you up.

MUM   I wasn't asleep.

ANNIE   Can I take the ...

MUM   I'm not done yet.

ANNIE   Oh. Okay.

MUM   Have you had your bath?

ANNIE   Yes.

MUM   Was there enough water?

ANNIE   Yes, there was plenty.

MUM   Did / you piss in

ANNIE   No.

MUM   It's a cunt / to

ANNIE   It's a cunt to clean oh I know.

MUM   Watch your mouth.

ANNIE   Where's Dad again?

MUM   You think he tells me where he goes?

ANNIE   Mum?

MUM   Yes?

ANNIE   Do you think he is avoiding me?

MUM   Come here.

ANNIE   *(wipes her own mouth)* I'm fine.

MUM   Oh.

ANNIE   Thank you.

MUM   So ... what did they say about the weather?

ANNIE   -

MUM   On the radio?

ANNIE   They said it will be ... nice.

MUM   What do you mean nice? What kind of - nice?

ANNIE   You know, kind of warmish but not too hot ... there was a few drops of rain during the night but nothing too heavy, actually I think they said it might be perfect for the crops.

MUM   Tz, tz, tz.

ANNIE   Jesus fucking Christ!

MUM   Annie.

ANNIE   Tell me. What's wrong with the weather now?

MUM   Well that cant be good, can it? You know what they say: "Till April's dead, change not a thread".

ANNIE   Who says that?

MUM   It means we could still get frost. And that's / worst

ANNIE   Worst for the crops.

MUM   Yes, frost and strong winds.

ANNIE   It kills them. Yes. Well, it's nice to know what kills them. Might come in handy one day. Thank you (very much).

MUM   I'm just saying.

ANNIE   Of course you are just saying.

MUM   Aunt Marie would know about it.

ANNIE   I bet she would.

MUM   You should ask her about it.

ANNIE   I will.

MUM   How is she anyway?

ANNIE   -

MUM   What?

ANNIE   I don't really know.

MUM   Didn't you go to see her this week?

ANNIE   No.

MUM   Oh. You really should.

ANNIE   Then I did.

MUM   When?

ANNIE   Last night.

MUM   I hope you didn't stay late. You know they don't like people coming too late.

ANNIE   Actually now when I think about it – it was this morning. I went to see them this morning.

MUM   I hope you didn't barge in while they were having their breakfast. You know how uncle George likes his Sunday breakfast.

ANNIE   Actually, when I really think about it, when I think about it very carefully – I didn't go to see them at all. In fact I phoned last night. Just before they had their tea. At a decent time. They were very happy to talk to me. And we didn't talk for more than ah well I don't know say 5, maybe 10 minutes.

MUM   Ach. What's phone. You should really go and visit sometimes.

ANNIE   -
Should I?

MUM   Yes.

ANNIE   -
Fine.

MUM   You and Mark.

ANNIE   What about me and Mark?

MUM   You could go together.

ANNIE   -
Okay.

MUM   Couldn't you?

ANNIE   I don't know. Possibly.

MUM   Why wouldn't you?

ANNIE   All sorts of reasons, Mum.

MUM   You are still together though, aren't you?

ANNIE   I don't know.
         Would you like us to be?

MUM   Now what kind of question is that?

ANNIE   How's your chest today?

MUM   Ach.

ANNIE   Better?

MUM   I'm still alive.

ANNIE   Oh yes you are.

MUM   And what did she say?

ANNIE   Who?

MUM   Aunt Marie. On the phone.

ANNIE   Not much.

MUM   Is she well?

ANNIE   She asked about you.

MUM   And what did you tell her?

ANNIE   She said she came to see you the other day.

MUM   No-o.

ANNIE   She did. On Monday.

MUM   She made that up.

ANNIE   She said she was standing there knocking for more than
         10 minutes. And nothing.

MUM   I didn't hear anything.

ANNIE   Were you home on Monday?

MUM   Where else would I be?

ANNIE   I don't know … Were you maybe having a little nap?

MUM   You know I don't sleep during the day.

ANNIE   So how come you didn't hear her?

MUM   I'm telling you she made that up.

ANNIE   Why would she do that?

MUM   Just to annoy me. That's what she does. She never liked
         me.

ANNIE   She is just worried about you.

MUM   Then she should come and visit sometimes.

ANNIE   Jesus Mum.

MUM   Well I can't go there, can I?

ANNIE   You are not that ill.

MUM   And how do you imagine me getting there?

ANNIE   Well, you put on your coat and kind of go … that way.

MUM   Don't be ridiculous. I can't walk all the way to theirs.

ANNIE   I'll drive you.

MUM   Oh no, thank you very much.

ANNIE   What now?

MUM   I don't like the way you drive.

ANNIE   You've never seen me drive.

MUM   I've seen you ride your bike.

ANNIE   What, when I was twelve?

MUM   Let's just say it didn't fill me with confidence.

ANNIE   Fine.

MUM   I'm just saying …

ANNIE   I said fine. You don't have to.

MUM   Annie.

ANNIE   I don't care. I really don't care.

MUM   It's just not …

ANNIE   What?

MUM   Maybe next time.

ANNIE   Always "next time". What if there is no next time?

MUM   Well I can't go just right now.

ANNIE   Why not? Tell me? What's the reason now?

MUM   I don't feel too well.

ANNIE   What, is there something stuck? There?

MUM   Why are you talking to me like that?

ANNIE   I don't believe this.

MUM   I didn't mean to upset you.

ANNIE   I ... I can't. You know what ... I just can't, Mum.
          When's Dad coming home?

MUM   I don't know. He never tells me anything. No one does.

ANNIE   I want to talk to him.

MUM   Are you upset now?

ANNIE   No.

MUM   It's just my ...

ANNIE   I can't. I have to ...

MUM   Don't go.

ANNIE   I need to make some tea.

MUM   Don't go right now.

ANNIE   Would you like a cup?

MUM   If you are making it.

ANNIE   Well, in fact I'm not.

MUM   Annie please don't yell.

ANNIE   Well I'm not making it.

MUM   Why did you ask me then?

ANNIE   I'm not making it for myself, but I will make it for you
         if you want it, that's what I'm asking, would you like
         a cup of tea, weather I'm making it or not. Would *you*
         like *me* to make you a cup of tea? It's that simple. And
         it's not a problem, I don't mind, and I wouldn't be
         asking it if it was a problem.

MUM   -

ANNIE   So?

*MUM drops her mug of tea and it spills into her lap. She coughs a bit and
puts a hand to her chest, there is something stuck in her throat.*

ANNIE   What now?

MUM coughs. Whatever was stuck gives a bit.

ANNIE   Mum?

MUM   I'm fine.

ANNIE   What was it?

MUM   Nothing.

ANNIE   Sure?

MUM   Yes.

ANNIE   So. Tea?

MUM   Yes please.

MUM hands her the mug she was holding.
ANNIE takes it.

MUM   Thank you.

ANNIE   You are welcome.

ANNIE leaves to make the tea.

Scene 4

Mum is still sitting in the chair.
She is awake.
Annie comes in carrying one cup of tea.

MUM   (Oh) there you are.

ANNIE   Hi.

MUM   Hi.

ANNIE   Tea.

MUM   That's nice.

ANNIE doesn't give tea to Mum but sips from the mug herself.

ANNIE   I've just had a bath.

MUM   Good.
           Was it nice?

ANNIE   Yes. It was.

MUM   Good.

ANNIE   I used your salts.

MUM   They are nice, aren't they?

ANNIE   Yes.
           -
           They smell like you.

MUM   Thank you.

ANNIE   And then I had a shower.

MUM   Was there enough hot water?

ANNIE   Yes. Plenty.

MUM   Good. Good.

ANNIE   And then I had a little pee in the shower.

MUM   Oh well that's all right. It's all just water anyway, isn't it?

ANNIE   But I scrubbed.

MUM   You didn't have too.

ANNIE   And now Dad is making me breakfast.

MUM   Were there any eggs in the fridge?

ANNIE   Yes. He went to the shop.
          He got us papers. And bread. Some juice.
          And now we will have breakfast. The two of us.

MUM   Oh. That's nice.

ANNIE   Yes.

MUM smiles.

ANNIE   Can I ... Can I ask you something?

MUM   Of course.

ANNIE   Are you …

MUM   Yes?

ANNIE   Are you happy?

MUM   That's a funny question.

ANNIE   Why?

MUM   I don't know.

ANNIE   Are you?

MUM   Right now?

ANNIE   Yes.

MUM   I would have to think about it.

ANNIE   It's …

MUM   -

ANNIE   It's different.

MUM   Yes.

ANNIE   We talk.

MUM   Yes.

ANNIE   It's odd.

MUM   But nice.

ANNIE   But odd.

MUM   Do you ... do you mind talking?

ANNIE   No, not at all. Actually, I think I really like it.
          It's just ...

MUM   I know.

ANNIE   I have so much to ask.

MUM   Go on.

ANNIE   No.

MUM   Why not?

ANNIE   I don't know. It's too early.

MUM   No. It's fine.

ANNIE   Really?

MUM   I don't know. We can try. See what happens.
          Go on.

ANNIE   Okay ...
          Why ... why did you stop going to aunt Marie's?

MUM   She would have known. She was my sister. She would
          have known at once.

ANNIE   You think so?

MUM   Yes. She could always tell. (It's the) same blood.

ANNIE   And you didn't want her to know?

MUM   No.

ANNIE   Why? Why didn't you want anyone to know?

MUM   You would have just worried. All of you. And that
          wouldn't help anyone.

ANNIE   But you knew?

MUM   Yes.

ANNIE   How long?

MUM   A while.

ANNIE   How long Mum?

MUM   Six months.

ANNIE   Mum, you should / have told

MUM   Is it my turn now?

ANNIE   What?

MUM   I have a few questions I'd like to ask. If that's all right?

ANNIE   -
          Well … Sure.

MUM   How is Mark?

ANNIE   -

MUM   Is he all right?

ANNIE   Mark's gone.

MUM   You or him?

ANNIE   Him?

MUM   Why?

ANNIE   I think he got bored with me.

MUM   Did you love him?

ANNIE   Yes.

MUM   Do you still love him?

ANNIE   I do.
         Very much.

MUM   I'm sorry.

ANNIE   Did you love Dad?

MUM   I did. When I was younger.

ANNIE   And later?

MUM   We got used to each other.

ANNIE   Did you ever think of leaving him?

MUM   No.

ANNIE   Do you think he ever thought of that?

MUM   He left once. He was gone for almost a year.

ANNIE   I didn't know.

MUM   You were too young.
Do you like your job?

ANNIE   I do.
Did you like yours?

MUM   Never. I thought kids were always just a bit too loud.
Do you like living alone?

ANNIE   No. Not at all.
Did you like uncle George?

MUM   I slept with him before he married your aunt.

ANNIE   Mum.

MUM   She doesn't know, so you better watch your mouth. All
right?

ANNIE   All right.

MUM   Are you happy?

ANNIE   No. Not right now.
Are you scared?

MUM   No. Not any more.
Do you drink on your own?

ANNIE   Sometimes I do.

MUM   Why?

ANNIE   If I think Mark is not coming back.
          And since you died.

MUM   Does it make you feel better?

ANNIE   No. It makes me sick. Then I throw up.
          Did you ever drink?

MUM   Yes.

ANNIE   On your own?

MUM   Sometimes. When your Dad was gone. And after you
          moved out.

ANNIE   Did it make you feel better.

MUM   For a moment. Yes.

ANNIE   Did it hurt? You know. When you died?

MUM   No.

ANNIE   What did it feel like?

MUM   It was new. Feeling I've never had before. First it felt
          like something got stuck in my throat. And it grew this
          time. And I couldn't cough it up.
          -
          It felt like it would take a while.

ANNIE   Did it?

MUM   Yes.

ANNIE   How long?

MUM   To me it seemed like hours.

ANNIE   Did you know what it was?
         Did you know you were dying?

MUM   Yes. You know when it comes.

ANNIE   Why didn't you call me?

MUM   There was nothing you could've done.

ANNIE   But if I hadn't left … you know, if I hadn't left the room,
         to make the tea.

MUM   No. It was my time.

ANNIE   -
         I'm so sorry Mum.

MUM   You are still angry?

ANNIE   Yes.
         -
         I think so.

MUM   Who with?

ANNIE   You. Mark. Dad. Myself. Everyone.

MUM   For what?

ANNIE   -
          I don't know.
          -
          Were you angry?

MUM   Oh yes.

ANNIE   Who with?

MUM   I don't know. Same. Everyone. Anyone.

ANNIE   Why?

MUM   For being old. I guess. And ill.

ANNIE   What made you angry about it?

MUM   I don't think I deserved it.

ANNIE   I see.

MUM   Do you think I did?

ANNIE   No.

MUM   Do you think it changed me?

ANNIE   Yes.

MUM   How?

ANNIE   You became even angrier ... you became mean.

MUM   Did you wonder why?

ANNIE   Sometimes.

MUM   And? Did you ever find out?

ANNIE   I think I did.

MUM   So? Why?

ANNIE   I'm still not sure.
         It could've been all that waste and poison that couldn't
         leave your body.

MUM   Or?

ANNIE   Or - maybe you were always a bit selfish and mean and
         I just didn't notice it because I'm your daughter and it's
         hard to notice those things in a parent.

MUM   And?
         Which do you think it was?

ANNIE   -

MUM   -

ANNIE   I don't know.
         -
         Which one do you think it was?

MUM   -
         I don't know either.
         It's been going on for too long.

ANNIE	-
MUM	-
DAD	(*off*) Annie.
ANNIE	I will have to go soon.
MUM	I know.
ANNIE	Can I get you anything before I go?
MUM	No. I'm fine.
ANNIE	Tea?
MUM	No. Thank you.
ANNIE	Sure?
MUM	Yes.
ANNIE	Okay. I better …
MUM	…
ANNIE	I have to go and have breakfast.
MUM	…
ANNIE	I think it might be ready.
MUM	…
ANNIE	Dad's making it for me.

MUM   …

ANNIE   I have to go.

Voice from outside.

DAD   Annie?

ANNIE doesn't move.

DAD   Annie!

Blackout

End.

A PRAYER

by Selma Dimitrijevic

Between 2010 and 2015 directed by Lorne Campbell and Selma Dimitrijevic

Creative Collaborator/Designer: Garance Marneur

Originally Performed by Sandy Grierson at Northern Stage and Young Vic. At Hull Truck Theatre and Northern Stage performed by Scott Turnbull, at the Almeida, Young Vic and caravan showcase performed by Elspeth Brodie.

The original production of A Prayer was first co-commissioned and produced by Oran Mor as part of its A Play, A Pie and A Pint spring season 2010. The project was further developed at Northern Stage, Newcastle after winning the Title Pending Award, the award for the most innovative, thoughtful and intriguing proposal for a new piece of theatre.

This is June 2011 draft. We expect the play will change with every actor that performs it. Hopefully it will change often and profoundly.

Notes On The Greyscale Production Of *A PRAYER*

We have been performing A PRAYER since 2010 and we will continue as long as it seems interesting to our audiences.

It all started with Sandy Grierson, Garance Marneur, Lorne Campbell and Selma Dimitrijevic creating a half an hour version for a lunch time theatre in Glasgow (thanks to the wonderful artist, human and maverick David MacLennan).

It didn't go terribly well. A lot of people didn't like it.

But, some people loved it and some people wrote about it (thank you Gareth K Vile) and we kept working on it until Northern Stage saw something interesting in it and gave us TITLE PENDING award to go and make it better.

So we worked on it some more. And made it better.

Eventually Scott Turnbull took over from Sandy, and Selma took over from Lorne. Then Elspeth Brodie took over from Scott and we had our first female atheist. We also introduced a couple of songs.

During that time, we performed the show: in a children's theatre at the Theatre Royal Bath, 500 seat auditorium at Northern Stage, a conference room at the Young Vic, a dressing room at the Almeida theatre, a rehearsal room at the Hull Truck theatre, studio space at the Young Vic, cabaret space at Northern Stage, fringe theatre in Bristol and more than once in our front room. At least two of the performers were naked at some point in the show, and one of them unexpectedly did the whole show without any clothes (yes, you, Sandy Grierson), at the Almeida we had a BSL interpreter and we wished we could have her with us all the time; and in one of the very early versions, a lovely boy unexpectedly joined Sandy on stage and proceeded to teach him how to play Snap! The show was about 10 minutes longer than usual, and the boy's mother was petrified, but we loved it.

We find it works best when the actor plays M. And the audience are God.

We didn't tell our audience much about the show, but we did tell them we might talk to them.

We find we like it when the actor sticks to the lines as much as they can.

Except in the section between "So ... I'm in New York. In a hotel, on my own, I've never been there before." (pg 75) and "And I won't have a chance to tell her ... that she is wrong." (pg 79) which is more or less improvised during the show, and the details of the story change depending on which actor plays M.

We also feel it's no fun rehearsing this without an audience. Our family, neighbours, colleagues, friends, dogs ... they all sat through a lot of our rehearsals, and they all made a wonderful and strange God.

But ...

Feel free to use this text for your own version of the show.

Feel free to use it any way you want.

You can stage it as it is, or re-imagine the whole thing.

You can find a new and better way of having God in the room.

You can think about our stage directions or ignore them completely.

You can have no actors or several actors playing M.

Or like us, you can just have a woman or a man.

You can sing the whole thing, or put it on the radio.

Or you can do whatever else you think your audience might find interesting.

If you have questions we will do our best to answer.

We are not asking for any money

But we ask for a credit for the company.

If you have photos send us a few and we will put them on our website.

If we can we will come and see it.

Let us know how it goes.

Have fun!
Greyscale x

Rights now held by Samuel French.

A PRAYER

Characters

M   any gender, any age, any race.

M is looking at God.
God is looking at M.
How funny.
It feels as if the air is bit thinner, and breathing is easier and things are clearer.
It feels confusingly joyous.
All sorts of thoughts are going through M's mind.
Then M does something.
And then some more things go through M's mind.
And then - after some time - M speaks to God.

M   Hello.

If there is no answer, M speaks again. It's not like he was expecting a reaction anyway.

(M   Hello.)

If there is an answer, if God speaks back, it's almost too much for M to take it.
M reacts to it and it takes him a few seconds to recover. Maybe a bit longer. Maybe much longer.
God is still looking at him.
M has never experienced this before.
It's huge.

M   Sorry.

Pause.
Things are going through M's mind.

M   I'm just a bit, mhmm, you know.

Was M going to say "scared" or " too excited"?

M   This is a bit weird.

M looks carefully.
It definitely is God.

M   Weird.

God is looking at M. Patiently.
Then suddenly, without any warning, all cynicism disappears just for a few moments.
It feels amazing. So, so good.
It's kind of dizzying in a good, calm way.
M smiles. God probably smiles back.
It doesn't last too long.
M is not sure what just happened. He is not even sure that something happened.
Does the feeling go away? Does it hang about for a while?
On the other side of the room, M notices something. It's something he wants right now (like his glass of water and he really, really needs a sip now, or his towel if he just came out of the shower).
He decides to go for it.

M   If I could just…

He goes towards the other side of the room.
Very carefully.
If God moves out of his way, M thanks God.

M   Thank you.

Not being able to turn his back to God, or to take his eyes of God, but not very comfortable about getting too close either.
If M needs to get through God, he says things like:

M   Excuse me

I'll just, yes, thank you.

Eventually M takes a sip / finds the towel / gets his clothes / does whatever else was he doing.
M is not sure what to do with God.
Does she wait for a few moments for God to do something?

M   Okay, weird.

God doesn't do much.
Does M wait for a few seconds.

M   Are you going to say something?

Does God speak? Does God nod or give any other sign?
If God speaks, it's amazing and exciting.
M was a bit more prepared for it this time.

M   Okay.

Is M confused about how God got in there?

M   I thought I was maybe imagining …
           you know … this.

Something.

M   But I'm not, am I?

Is M saying this or asking a question? Does he know which one is it?

M   You are here.

Is there any answer from God?

(M   Literally here.)

There is an answer, of some kind. A sign.

M   Really?

M still needs the proof.
He knows how he could get it but is not sure how to ask.

M   Would you mind if I check?

What's the best way to put this?

M   Can I touch you?

Does God give M a sign?

M   Okay.

M is going to do it.

M   Okay. Here it is.

M is getting closer to God.
He is about to touch God.
This is pretty intense.
And …
M touches God.
Wow.
Fuck.

M   Wow.

God seems to be all right with this.

M   Fuck me /
                 sorry.

God doesn't seem to mind M swearing. God even finds it amusing.
Which was somewhat expected.

M   I just wanted to check.

Does checking seem ridiculous now?
Or does it make perfect sense?
What can M do to say thank you for this, to return the favour?

M   Do you want to touch me?

That seems only fair.
God gives M a sign. Maybe God even says "Yes" out loud. M is getting
slowly used to the voice of God.

M   All right.

This is exciting.
Very exciting.
M offers herself to be touched by God.
God touches M.

M   Wow. (*or some other non-sweary interjection*)

What is M's reaction? How big is his reaction? How does it feel?

M   Okay.
                 Okay.

This was pretty huge. And weird.

M   I just wanted to make sure (that) you are really here.

Something.

M   And you are.

Something.

M   You see, the thing is, the thing is …

This is very, very confusing.
And pretty funny.

M   I never thought you are real.

That's true.

M   And now you seem to be here.

That seems true too.

M   And also – you don't look like, you don't really look like
    how …

Hmmmm.

M   I never imagined you would look like this.

Something.

M   I mean I never imagined you at all, but if I did, I would
    have imagined, something a bit more …

M tries to describe what she means.

M   But not …

Something.

M   Fuck me / sorry.
           You see, I don't know how to – do this.

Something.

M   I mean, How did …
           Where did you come from?

Does God tell M where God came from? Is God telling the truth?
Did different parts of God come from different places. If yes. M can ask:

M   I see.
           That's weird.
           So does that mean you can be in many places at the
           same time?

If God doesn't come from many places M still thinks that's cool.

M   That's cool.

M enjoys this.

M   And
           Do you always look like this?

Is there a simple Yes or No answer?

M   Nice.

Something.

M   And do you … do this often?

God may be saying yes. God may be saying no. Either of those things might be a lie.

M   And do you know things, before they happen?

M takes out a coin.

M   Heads or tails?

God replies. God makes a choice.
M flips the coin.

M   Okay.

Something. God either got it right or not.

M   And can you
               make things go …
               (*sound for things being destroyed?*)
               you know
               destroy them?

M takes a biscuit / a grape / something small and easily destructible and offers it to God to destroy.

M   If you wanted to. Can you destroy this?

M is inviting God to destroy it.
What does God do?
Does God destroy it?
God probably does.

M   I see.

Something.

M   And how about about this?

M puts something else in front of God for God to destroy it.
An orange? Something a bit bigger but still easy to destroy.
Does God do it? Possibly.
M continues putting more and more valuable things in front of God.
Every time M aits for God to destroy it before offering the next object.
A bit of paper with a child's drawing on it? A book? Reading glasses? Debit card?
It might go on for a while…
But finally, after an offer from M, God doesn't do anything.
There is something God doesn't want to/can't destroy.

M   All right.

M feels like someone has just proved something, but she's not very clear on who or what.

M   All right.
                Not – how I imagined you.
                Not at all.

These revelations are very intriguing to M. And quite exciting.

M   And does it …

M removes what was left after God's last destruction and leaves the empty space in front of God.

M   Does it work
                the other way
                around?
                Can you

M is not trying to outsmart God.

M   Can you make things, make something.

M is inviting God to create something.

M   Out of this?

What does God do?
Does God Create something.
Does God even try?
Is God refusing to be tested like this?
One of those things happens.
And when it does it's obvious it's the only possible outcome.
Does it make M laugh?
There seems to be a strange understanding between M and God at the
moment. It makes them both feel pretty good. And pretty smart for some
reason.

M   Can you show me?

M is even more comfortable, still probably wouldn't touch God casually but
is not afraid to move any more.
If God creates something or even if God says yes.

M   That's amazing. Really amazing.
             So weird.

Something.

M   Because you see…
             I don't really believe in God.
             I never believed in you. Never.
             Because, it doesn't / it didn't
             it never seemed very – logical.
             To me. It never seemed very - intelligent.

Does this offend God in any way?

M   I'm sorry about that.

Something.

M   But I was never ever told you might be this.

          You seem kind and funny and sweet. And you wear nice shoes. And you laugh at things I say. And you seem to really listen to what I say.

          From what I was told you are this huge and scary, and jealous, and
          stubborn, this manipulative and homophobic and petty and cruel thing.

          Because that's what people say. The stories, that's what they make you
          sound like.

          And I just thought I always thought, that doesn't sound very Godly.
          No. That sounds Human.

M never put this into words before. He never thought he would.
Does it feel like he is finally talking to someone who might understand him.

M   Do you know what I mean?

M is not even contemplating how complex "do you know what I mean"
question might be. And he doesn't have to.

M   But now you are here I'm just confused, I'm not sure if you are

Is that what you, I mean
Are you stubborn?

What does God say to this?

M   (Are you) Jealous?

Does God reply?

M   Petty?
           Cruel?

This is a bit much for M. How is his mind dealing with all this.

M   Okay.

This is a scary thought.

M   And, are you here to do something to me?

Something. If the answers is no that's a huge relief.

M   Okay, good. So are you here so I can do something for
           you?

Something.

M   Well I'm, not sure I can do much.

Something.

M   I mean, I don't really know how to pray.
           No. (Sorry.)
           I might remember a line or two of Our Father
           But probably not in the right order

And I'm not sure if I can, you know, mean it.
So it doesn't seem worth doing it.
Really.

Is M looking for clues from God. God is not giving him any clues at the moment.

M   And I don't know any other prayers. You know, if you are
           not that God.

Oh, this is getting more and more complicated.

M   No, you are definitely not that God.

M is genuinely asking these questions which are not questions.

M   Now I know even less about what I can offer you.

Is M going to try any of this?

M   What about …

Something.

M   Do you want me to kneel for you?

God probably says yes or no. Does M try?

M   Shall I bow for you?
           Okay.
           Would you want me to hurt myself for you?

Something.

M   No, you don't look like that kind of God either.
      You are actually …

M looks carefully at God, he hasn't really noticed until now.

M   You're actually quite pretty.

Is that M flirting with God? God blushes.

M   How about, would you want me to sing for you?

M sings a song for God.
Does God enjoy it. Does God join in.
Either way M enjoys it.

M   That was fun.

Something.

M   So God.
      I guess people ask you for things a lot. Do they?

Do they?

M   Thought so.
      I really don't want to take advantage of you in any way.

      But I may never find myself in a position like this again,
      and there's something I would really like to know.

      So. May I ask you a question?

Something.

M   Do you know what I'm talking about?

God probably doesn't. But then again you never know.

M   It is the strangest thing that ever happened to me.
Apart from this.

Something.

M   So ... I'm in New York. In a hotel, on my own, I've
never been there before.
And I couldn't sleep, the time was all wrong, it was too
early, or maybe too late, and I was awake when I should
have been asleep, so I went out.

Something

M   I went out to this bar, this bar where they played jazz,
and it wasn't like *The Carlyle* or anything like that, it
was just a stupid little bar, where four guys played
jazz, sitting on those funny high stools, and one of
them holding the chubby guitar, and a few men ... few
people just sitting around because it was too late to go
anywhere else.
So I walked in, I walked down, and sat at the bar, not
looking around, looked past the barmen ...

*God might offer more details of the night, or correct M about how it
happened.*

M   A friendly guy, I looked to the row of bottles, whiskeys
he had right next to the wall, and I ordered one.
And as he was taking the bottle down, I saw in the
mirror behind the bottles, behind the barmen, behind
the bar I saw a woman.
A woman looking straight at me. Seeing me looking at
her. Definitely seeing me looking at her. And then she

smiled.

Which was odd. Really odd.

Because women usual don't smile at me like that. Not if they don't know me and I'm sitting in a strange city and in a strange bar.

Something.

M   So I drank my whiskey. And then – I guess I was just curious – I ordered another one, and there she was. She was still looking at me.

So I turned around.....And she smiled. And you know, I smiled.

And she said hello.

Hello.

And we started talking, and we talked all evening, all night.

And it was just easy.

It was at the same time the hardest and the easiest thing I've ever done, and it felt like we were doing it together and we knew how incredible, how unbelievable it is that this is how it feels to both of us.

It was just perfect.

Something.

M   And when it was time to leave the bar, she said she lived just around the corner and that I should come up. And I said yes.

It didn't feel dirty, it didn't feel cheap, it just – made sense. There was a logic, it was just so comfortable, so ... nice.

We went up.

We talked all night.

We kissed.

We made love.
We talked some more.
And …
And laughed at how obvious it all is, you know.
How easy it is to talk, and we wondered why was …
you know, what was all the fuss about. Men and women
and trying to … when it seemed so easy, so ridiculously
easy to us, just now.
We both knew it. And we both knew that the other one
feels the same.
It was like …

God might offer what it was like. And God is absolutely right.

M   I woke up very early, because of the light, there was so
        much sun, sun and light coming into the room, and she
        was snoring, very gently, which was quite funny, but I
        didn't mind.
        I knew this wasn't going to finish just like that, we were
        just about to start something. So quietly, very, very
        quietly I got up, got dressed, I got my wallet, and my
        jacket and went out to buy us coffee and croissants.
        I was going to surprise her.
        It was going to be a perfect morning. Because that's
        what made sense.
        So I bought the coffee and croissants, four croissants,
        and then I bought flowers, which was a bit cheesy but I
        thought she would laugh, and I didn't really care much,
        because things were so perfect. Flowers made sense. I
        don't know. Somehow.
        And I was on my way back, to this amazing women,
        I was just one block from her building, from where I
        spent the night, and then as I turned the corner … I
        looked up and …

God might sense what is coming next and offer it to M. As before, God is absolutely right.

M   … the building wasn't there.
           It just wasn't there.
           And I thought I got it wrong, so I went back, a few
           streets back, with my coffee, and flowers, and chocolate
           croissants and then tried again, going straight back to
           her building.
           But it wasn't there.
           I didn't know the town.
           I've never been to New York before.
           I know all that.
           I could have taken the wrong turn.
           …
           But I didn't.
           I knew where I spent the night.
           I knew the building.
           And it wasn't there.

Does God know what happened to the building.

M   So I went back, again and again…
           I kept going back to the coffee shop and then again
           through the streets that should lead to her building but
           every time, every single time, I turned that corner, or
           eventually some other corner … it just … wasn't there.
           And then I realised.
           I know only her first name.
           Nothing else.
           I don't know where she works.
           I don't know any of her friends.
           I didn't know anything about her.
           Except that her and I – make sense.

Something.

M   And then I realised she was going to wake up, she was
going to wake up thinking she had this perfect night,
with someone who feels the same, with someone who
… gets her, she was going to wake up, just as I did,
thinking this is just the beginning of something huge,
of something real, and amazing, something she gave up
a long time ago …. and then she will realise I am not
there.
She will think … it was a one night stand for me.
She will think … it wasn't perfect. It wasn't easy.
She will think it was all a lie.
She will think I lied to her that night.
And I won't have a chance to tell her … that she is
wrong.

How does M go into asking the questions? What are the questions?

M   So if you can, if you know those things,
        …
        if you can destroy things, and create things

Does M mention things God destroyed or created just a few minutes ago?

M   and have powers, and meet prayers …
        if you have answers …

Something.

M   And you look like you do … you look so wise,
like you know so much about so many things.
If you do … can I just ask you.

Something.

M   (Do you think) I will …
           will I ever meet her again?
           (If I go back to New York?)

*God answers M's question. It might be yes or no or something completely
different bu M believes God knows the truth.
If God says yes, M has to ask:*

M   And will she, will she recognize me?

Does God say yes? If not does M leave?

M   And …

M has to ask just this last question.

M   … and will she know, that I am telling the truth, when I
           say I tried to find her, will she believe me … ?

Something.

M   Will she believe me?

*God gives M an answer.
And although huge, and odd, it feels good to know after all this time.*

M   I see.

*M is grateful for it.
M is grateful to God for answering his question.*

M   Thank you.
           Thank you.

End.